Guess the Order

By Brian Sargent

Consultants
Chalice Bennett
Elementary Specialist
Martin Luther King Jr. Laboratory School
Evanston, Illinois

Ari Ginsburg
Math Curriculum Specialist

Children's Press®
A Division of Scholastic Inc.
New York   Toronto   London   Auckland   Sydney
Mexico City   New Delhi   Hong Kong
Danbury, Connecticut

Designer: Herman Adler Design
Photo Researcher: Caroline Anderson
The photo on the cover shows a boy holding up photos of his cousin that
were taken at a carnival.

Library of Congress Cataloging-in-Publication Data

Sargent, Brian, 1969–
 Guess the order / by Brian Sargent.
  p. cm. — (Rookie read–about math)
 ISBN 0-516-24963-0 (lib. bdg.)   0-516-29809-7 (pbk.)
 1. Counting—Juvenile literature. 2. Problem solving—Juvenile
literature. I. Title. II. Series.
 QA113.S366 2006
 513.2'11—dc22
                                    2005019648

It's a box for me!
Who sent it to me?

The box is from my cousin, Jess.

A letter and photos came with it.

OPEN THIS LETTER FIRST

5

Dear Sam,
Here are five photos from my trip to the carnival. Can you put the photos in the right order?

Love,
Jess

The letter says, "Here are five photos from my trip to the carnival. Can you put the photos in the right order?"

Sure, I can do that!

I love to solve problems.

Let's look at the photos.

11

The first picture is easy.
Here Jess is waiting to buy
a ticket for the carnival.

That's photo number one.

The last picture is easy, too.

This shows Jess leaving the carnival. She has a giant dragon and her face is painted.

Since there are five photos, that one is photo number five.

How can I put the rest
of the photos in the right
order? I should look for
clues.

Aha! In every photo, Jess
has a butterfly on her face.

She must have had her
face painted first!

17

2

This photo must have been taken right after Jess got her ticket.

I'll call it photo number two.

Only two photos are left.

Here Jess is eating dinner.

Here she has just won
a dragon at a game booth.

Which came first?

Wait a minute! The dragon is sitting next to Jess when she's eating.

Jess must have won the dragon before dinner.

3

4

23

So now I know the order of the photos!

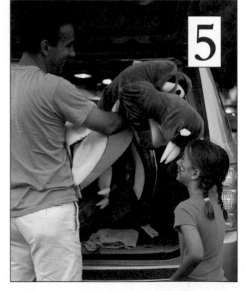

I solved the problem.

Now, I wonder what is in the box?

It's the dragon!

Thanks, Jess!

Words You Know

box

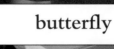

butterfly

carnival

dragon

leaving

letter

photo

waiting

Index

About the Author

Brian Sargent is a middle-school math teacher. He lives in Glen Ridge, New Jersey, with his wife Sharon and daughters Kathryn, Lila, and Victoria. He enjoys putting things in order.

Photo Credits